THOUGHTS
ON
LOVE

COLLECTOR'S EDITION
(BECAUSE YOU FOUND IT)

Written by: April Hill Writing
Illustrated by: April Hill Writing
Edited by: April Hill Writing

NOW ADAPTED INTO A MAJOR MOTION PICTURE.

All rights reserved.

You have the right to remain silent, it will not be held against you
in any court, not even a basketball court. The author has given
written permission to show this book to your grandparents to
make them smile. You may also use this book as tinder to start
a fire if stranded on an island after a plane crash. This book may
also serve use as a door stop, a paper weight, a weapon to stop
intruders, or ironically as part of a stand for your television when
you are too tired to read any longer. Any reference to human
hearts, eyes, the brain, beds, feelings, light-houses, aliens, ghosts,
the moon or stars are that of a work of fiction and not at all true or
scientifically reliable.

Thankyou for finding me a way to travel the earth while being
stranded in these pages. Thankyou for bringing me anywhere you
are right now, maybe a mountain, or a goat farm, or a tornado, or
a tomoato, or best yet bundled somewhere warm and cozy for the
night.

Mud St. Publishing's Library of Makabelieva

Writing, April Hill
        Thoughts On Love

p ekdf330m3pp1p1p1m2 (I. made)
03920 (th.3se. #num.ber.s#) ek3i2mq,2m2 (up) 29383810
(again). 343500350 (to2) e30920930 (seem) aj392928
(official.)99 911 9

Manufactured on Planet Earth, in reality 30-2aL40.

Also Available By April Hill Writing

APRIL HILL WRITING.
THOUGHTS ON LOVE.

©2019 April Hill Writing
©2019 Mud Street Publishing
@aprilhillwriting
aprilhillwriting@gmail.com

For Stanley,

Not you Stanley,

A different Stanley.

YOU   SHOWED   ME   THAT   YOU

RHYMES   WITH   LOVE

+   FOR   THAT   I'D   LOVE

TO   THANK   YOU.

COLD   MORNINGS

THE   FIRE   ROARING

THE   RAIN   IS   POURING

+   YOU   ARE   SNORING.

I'D TRAVEL THE WORLD FOR YOU,

BUT I'D MUCH RATHER

STAY BUNDLED IN BED.

I AM PIECES OF SAND

AT YOUR FEET

YOU ARE THE WAVES AT THE BEACH

CRASHING INTO ME.

You Make My
Alien Heart
Slow Down.

YOU MAKE MY LIFE

A BETTER HELL.

I   WOKE   UP

+

SHOOK   MY   EYELIDS,

YOU   WERE   STUCK   INSIDE   THEM.

Tossing
and turning,
chasing your face.
Running over rough spots
and the corners of my brain.
I woke up and shook
my eyelids
you were stuck inside them.

METAPHORS FOR OUR LOVE.

COMING IN FROM THE COLD.

TOO MUCH COFFEE.

WHISPERS YOU CAN MAKE SENSE OF.

I DON'T CONSIDER THIS ART

+ I DO NOT CONSIDER THIS GREAT,

BUT I CONSIDER YOU BOTH.

I DON'T KNOW IF

THERE IS SUCH A THING AS

TOO MUCH,

BUT IF THERE IS I KNOW

IT DOES NOT APPLY TO LOVE IN YOUR HEART

OR A GOOD THOUGHT IN YOUR BRAIN.

TAKE IT WITH ME

WHERE YOU GO

ME + YOU

WILL MAKE IT HOME.

PEOPLE FORGET

LOVE DOES NOT HAVE SKIN,

LOVE IS WITHIN.

I TRAVELLED THE WORLD.

WHAT WERE THE CHANCES

WE MET WITHIN GLANCES.

I AM SO LUCKY

TO HAVE YOU LOVE ME.

MY FAVOURITE PART OF MY DAY

IS YOU.

YOU MAKE IT HARD

TO HEAR ABOUT HEART-ACHE.

I MISS

SHARING YOUR AIR.

I like the things about you
that I do not like about myself.

I like the imperfection in your skin.
I like when your hair falls out.
I like the smell of your morning breath.
I like the way you look right before bed.
I like when you trip and fall.
I like when you burn food.
I like when you get angry with me.
I like when you make me smile.

I LIKE THE THINGS ABOUT YOU
THAT I DON'T LIKE
ABOUT MYSELF.

YOUR LOVE

SPEAKS MY LOVE.

MAY I BOTTLE YOUR SMELL?

MY LUNGS ARE

JUST NOT BIG ENOUGH.

THE SUN REFLECTS ONTO THE MOON,

I DON'T SHINE BRIGHT, THAT'S YOU.

I COULD BE CLEVER WITH MY WORDS

+ TELL YOU, YOU MUST HAVE BEEN

BORN BEFORE THE EARTH.

INSIST YOU ARE TIMELESS

+ THE EXPERIENCE IT MUST HAVE

TAKEN TO CRAFT YOUR EXISTENCE.

I WANT TO BE OPEN, SIMPLE + PLAIN

TO EMPHASIZE JUST HOW LUCKY I AM

THAT A TIMELESS BEAUTY

JUST AS PERFECT AS YOU,

EXISTS IN THE UNIVERSE

AT THE SAME TIME AS I DO.

BREAK THE HEART

✦ SET ME FREE.

I DIDN'T LIKE THE IDEA
OF NEEDING ANYTHING
MORE THAN I NEED YOU.

☺

YOUR FACE

IS MY HAPPY PLACE.

I WILL   RISK

YOUR   SICKNESS

IT   TASTES   GOOD

OFF   YOUR   LIPS.

I RESPECT YOUR OPINION

SO MUCH THAT

I AM ACTUALLY STARTING TO LIKE MYSELF.

YOU MAKE ME

FEEL ALRIGHT

BECAUSE YOU MAKE ME

FEEL LIKE THIS EVERYNIGHT.

I WANT YOU WITH ME WHEN I MESS UP,

NOT TO CATCH ME AS I FALL,

BUT TO BE THERE WHEN I GET BACK UP.

THE ONLY CONSTANT I NEED AFTER IT ALL.

IF YOU HAVE NOT LEARNED

TO LOVE THE ONES WHO HATE YOU,

YOU HAVE NOT LEARNED TO LOVE.

I see you and
I become a child again.
Finishing a report about something
I have no knowledge in.
Creating a story and
a somewhat happy ending
before even beginning
to put **ink** on a page.

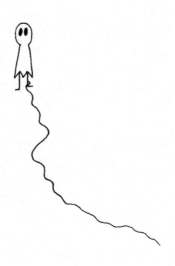

PIECES OF YOU

HANG OFF ME

LIKE THE LONGEST VINES

OR FILTHIEST LEAVES.

IT'S AN ODD FEELING

FEELING LIKE SOMEONES' FAVOURITE

WHEN YOUR FAVOURITE THING

IS THAT PERSON'S FEELINGS.

HERE I AM, ALL OF ME
EVERYTHING I AM YET,
HERE WE GROW, PERFECTLY,
EVER SINCE WE MET.

I AM NOT PERFECT,

BUT I HAVE A PERFECT PERSON.

♥

I LOVE YOU.

I HAVE TO.

IT DOESN'T MATTER

IF I WANT TO.

METAPHORS FOR OUR LOVE:

MY FEET MEETING A SILHOUETTE.

SLOW DANCING AT A WEDDING

(OURS OR OTHERWISE).

A DEVIL + ANGEL ON MY SHOULDERS,

BUT YOU ARE BOTH.

OUR LOVE IS A LIGHTHOUSE

CONSTANTLY SEARCHING FOR

EACH OTHER IN OUR DEPTHS.

you are the middle of the night,

descending stairs i've counted

a thousand times.

i'm at the bottom

+ catch a phantom flight

you take me one step further

than i've been all my life.

Here I lived.

Insomnia.

For You Do Not Fit In Dreams.

I ALWAYS TRY TO BE MYSELF

BUT I'M NEVER AS REAL

AS WHEN I'M HOLDING YOU.

YOU ARE MY RELIEF,

 MY REASON + MY RELEASE.

I LOVE THE WAY

YOU TELL THE STORY

OF HOW WE FELL IN LOVE.

CAN I MAKE A LIVING

OUT OF LOVING YOU?

Take the seaweed
with the sand.

Take the sky
with the land.

Take my heart
with my hand.

AT FIRST THOUGHT

IT SEEMS OFFENSIVE

TO TRAP OUR LOVE

INTO THREE LITTLE WORDS,

BUT WE TRAPPED A LOVE

THREE UNIVERSES WIDE

INTO TWO SILLY LITTLE BODIES.

BRUSHING OUR TEETH TOGETHER

MAKES ABSOLUTELY NO SENSE.

IT TAKES TWICE AS LONG

+ I GET IN YOUR WAY,

I CAN'T RINSE OUT MY MOUTH

+ YOU SPIT ON MY HAND,

BUT WITHOUT YOU I WOULD

HAVE NO REASON TO BRUSH

MY TEETH ANYWAYS.

YOU ARE FAR FAR AWAY,

BUT HERE IS WHERE YOU STAY.

♡ ♡

I AM AFRAID TO TELL YOU

JUST HOW MUCH I LOVE YOU

INCASE I LOSE YOU.

I READ IT IN A BOOK

OR SAW IT ON T.V.

A FACT ABOUT YOUR FACE

+ WHAT IT MEANS TO ME.

WE WENT TO SEE
A MUSIC SHOW
+ YOU WERE
THE ONLY SONG I REMEMBER.

I MISS YOU
WHEN I'M WITH YOU.
I MISS YOU
WHEN YOU'RE GONE.
NEVER LEAVE ME
WHEN YOU'RE WITH ME
YOU WERE WITH ME
ALL ALONG.

I AM NOT JUST LOVING TO LOVE,

LIKE I AM NOT JUST EATING TO SURVIVE.

I WANT TO TASTE IT IN EVERY BITE,

THAT YOU WANT TO PUT FLAVOUR

IN MY LIFE.

LET'S GET EXCITED

OVER THE LITTLE THINGS

THE MOVIES WE PICK

+ WHERE TO EAT DINNER,

THE MUSIC WE KISS TO

+ WHAT WE MIGHT DO.

YOUR   FAVOURITE THINGS

BECOME   MY   FAVOURITE THINGS,

BECAUSE   MY   FAVOURITE THING

IS   YOU.

I LONG FOR FEW THINGS,

THE SUN WHEN IT IS CLOUDY

+ YOU WHEN I AM SAD.

I FEEL STUCK IN AN OCEAN,

WITH NO METAPHOR,

TO SAY I LOVE YOU.

YOU SAY THE THINGS

MY BRAIN DOSN'T KNOW

THAT I KNOW.

THE MOMENT I MET YOU,

MY LIFE FLASHED BEFORE MY EYES.

I ALWAYS KNEW YOU WOULD BE

THE END OF MY LIFE.

YOU HAVE ME QUESTIONING

MY OWN EXISTENCE,

BECAUSE OF THE HAPPINESS

THAT SLEEPS BETWEEN US.

I AM TRYING TO LIVE

IN THE MOMENT,

BUT I CAN'T HELP

BUT DREAM OF MY

LIFE WITH YOU.

GO OUT + FIND SOMEONE

WHO MAKES YOU HAPPY

+ THEN FIND OUT

THAT THEY MAKE YOU HAPPIER.

SOME DEFINE LOVE AS DESIRE,

AFFECTION, LUST OR A SMILE,

REGRET, A TOUCH, A WALK, OR A CHILD.

SOME DEFINE LOVE IN MORE WORDS THAN I DO,

I DEFINE LOVE AS YOU.

I DON'T NEED THINGS

TO BE HAPPY,

I NEED YOU.

I love you to the moon,
not back though.
I want to live there
alone forever with you.
We can start
a little restaurant
where we serve moon rock milkshakes,
we can take day dates
to look down on the
earth as it quakes.
We can bake the stars
at five million degrees
and wonder why they
turned out so crispy.

I LOVE YOU TO THE MOON,

NOT BACK THOUGH.

I WANT TO LIVE THERE

ALONE FOREVER WITH YOU.

YOU   MAKE   ME

HAPPY

WHEN I   SHOULDN'T BE.

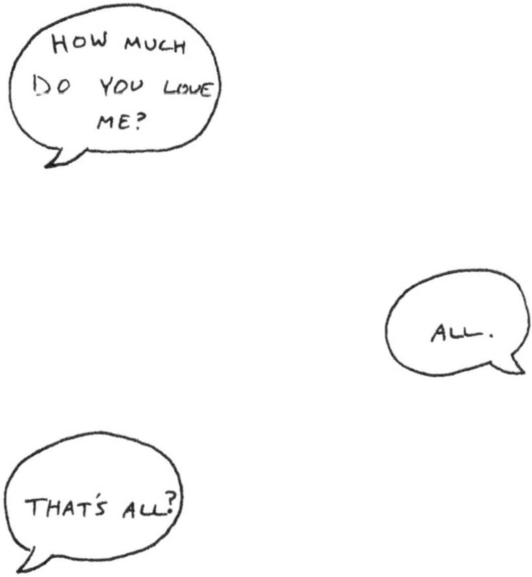
HOW MUCH DO YOU LOVE ME?
ALL.
THAT'S ALL?

YOU   ARE   SO   BEAUTIFUL

IN   THE   WAY   THAT

YOU   WILL   NEVER   LOVE   ME.

YOU FOLLOW YOUR DREAMS

& I WILL FOLLOW YOU.

BE WITH SOMEONE

WHO DOESN'T CARE IF

YOU WEAR VANS TO A WEDDING.

I CAN'T PROMISE YOU MUCH
BUT I WILL GIVE YOU
ALL THAT I CAN,
+ THAT MIGHT BE
THE ONLY PROMISE WORTH A DAMN.

YOU ARE A PLANET, WITH MOONS & STARS
& I CAN'T GO FAR.

I NEED TO BREATH YOUR ATMOSPHERE
& I ONLY GET IT WHEN I AM NEAR.

I COULD NOT SHARE YOU
WITH ANYONE ELSE,
I DON'T EVER WANT TO
LIVE IN THAT HELL.

I LIKE TO IMAGINE
SOMEONE PUTTING YOU TOGETHER
PIECE BY PIECE
SO CAREFULLY
& SO PERFECTLY.

TORN   BETWEEN

LOVING   YOU   WITH   ALL   MY   HEART

OR PLAYING IT SAFE UNTIL YOU REALIZE

I   AM   FALLING   APART.

BECAUSE IF I
CAN SEE YOUR EYES,
I CAN READ
YOUR MIND.

There is something in the way
you try and tell a lie
because if I can see your eyes,
I can read your mind.
There is something in the way
you look as time goes by
all that I see now
In the future you are mine.

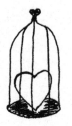

You can't

take my

love from me.

YOUR   SMILE   IS

THE   SUN

TOO   BRIGHT   TO   TOUCH .

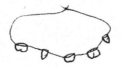

I HANDMADE YOU A PIECE OF ME.

I PULLED OUT ALL MY TEETH,

I TIED THEM UP

& SET THEM FREE.

THEY LIVE ON IN MEMORY

LEARNING HOW TO BE HAPPY.

I WANTED TO MAKE YOU SMILE.

IF WE MET AT A DIFFERENT TIME IN OUR LIVES

THINGS WOULD HAVE TURNED OUT DIFFERENT.

I MEAN, THE END RESULT WOULD BE THE SAME,

BUT THE EVENTS WOULD BE DIFFERENT.

NOT BETTER + NOT WORSE,

JUST A DIFFERENT LOVE.

METAPHORS FOR OUR LOVE:

YOU ARE A TREE FALLING IN A FOREST
+ I AM ALWAYS AROUND TO HEAR YOUR SOUND.

BOOMERANG LOVE; YOU MUST LEAVE
AS I STAY HERE BURNING UP.

THIS HAS BECOME BOILING WATER,
WAITING TO CYCLE BACK DOWN + AROUND.

YOU ARE MY TOMORROW,
ALWAYS A TAD TOO FAR AWAY TODAY.

THATS THE THING ABOUT LOVE,

IT CAN HAPPEN EASY

OR IT CAN HAPPEN HARD,

BUT STAYING IN LOVE

SHOULD BE YOUR FAVORITE PART.

Hold my breath
and count to four thousand.
Run a little bit
on the pavement.
Wash my hands
one hundred times.
Cut some
almost ripened limes.
Eat some toast,
clean out my closet.
Talk to a ghost.
Carve a roast.

Whatever passes the days
until you and
I find a way.

WHATEVER PASSES THE DAYS

UNTIL YOU + I FIND A WAY.

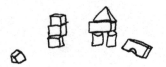

I AM STACKING BLOCKS

YOU ARE KNOCKING THEM OVER.

I am putting pieces
of a puzzle together
on your coffee table
with a broken leg.

I am painting
you a portrait
with washable paint.

I am stacking blocks
you are
knocking them over.

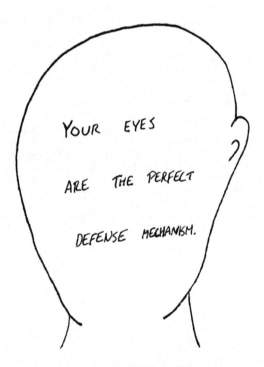

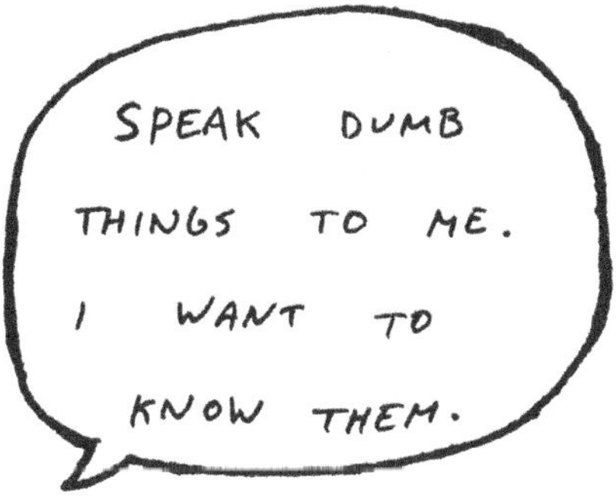
SPEAK DUMB THINGS TO ME. I WANT TO KNOW THEM.

I want to talk about
what's wrong with the world
with you:

The oceans are turning to muck.

The sky seems to smell weird.

There is poison in the people.

Some guy spit on my car window.

Someone kicked me in the leg.

I still like people.

I WANT   TO   TALK   ABOUT

WHAT'S   WRONG   WITH   THE   WORLD

WITH   YOU.

YOU   DREW   A   HEART

IN   THE DUST ON MY SHELF

SO I NEVER   CLEANED UP MY HOUSE.

MOST   DAYS

I DON'T WORRY OVER TYING MY SHOES

+ I DON'T WORRY OVER LOVING YOU.

MY FOREARMS WILL BURN

WITH THE WEIGHT

OF YOUR POSSIBILITY.

You are not
a ghost in your body.
I can not catch you.
Float face up in
my sore palms
for what feels like eternity.
My forearms will burn
with the weight of
your possibility.
Sink low
into a lonely rocking chair.
Watching you
run and jump
through the gathered grass.

MY HEART SKIPPED

EVERY THIRD BEAT

UNTIL YOU CAME &

FILLED IT FOR ME.

I want to make you
as glad as I am mad.

I want to make you
as good as I am bad.

I want to make you
as happy as I am sad.

:)

I WANT TO MAKE YOU

AS HAPPY AS

I AM SAD.

YOU MIGHT BE UP IN SOME HEAVEN
OR JUST DOWN IN SOME DIRT,
ALIVE, IN MY LIFE, OR ACROSS THE EARTH,
I PROMISE, 'I'M WITH YOU.'
I WHISPER, 'I SWEAR,'
'MY MIND IS NOT MINE
WHEN YOU ARE NOT HERE.'

I AM UNABLE TO FULLY GRASP

THE IDEA OF LOVING YOU.

I WILL NEVER LOVE YOU ENOUGH

+ THAT'S THE TRUTH.

TWO BEATING HEARTS

HEARD ABOVE A BREATH,

SYNCED UP TO FILL

THE SILENCE BETWEEN I LOVE YOU'S.

As quiet as it is dark.
I would lay and listen
to a drip from the kitchen.
I would sit and stare
at shadows that circled my eyes.
When I closed them,
it was more swirls in my stomach.
I could hear birds,
or owls,
or monsters outside.
Unable to sleep right at night
Now the noise
outweighs it all.
Two beating hearts
heard above a breath
synced up to fill
the silence between
I love you's

YOU BRING OUT

THE WORST IN ME

THEN YOU LOVE IT.

OUR   MINDS   GET   DARK

LETS   TRY   &   FIND   EACHOTHER

IN   THE   NIGHT.

I think you are lovely.
Full of everything somebody could want.
How perfect if that person was me.

I think you are lovely.
Your hair falls nicely,
your smile is wrong in just the right ways.

I think you are lovely.
Either you are lovely,
or I am lonely.

EITHER YOU ARE LOVELY

OR I AM LONELY.

METAPHORS FOR OUR LOVE:

YOU ARE COLD SHEETS

ON A WINTER NIGHT.

YOU ARE WET FEET

AFTER A RAINY WALK.

YOU ARE THE MOMENTS

BEFORE SO MUCH WARMTH.

PRACTICE MAKES PERFECT

SO PRACTICE MAKES YOU.

SUCH A SIMPLE IDEA

ME & YOU.

IT BREAKS MY HEART

THE POSSIBILITY THAT

I MIGHT NOT BE THE PERSON

WHO CAN LOVE YOU BEST.

Folded under layers of dirt,
a mess filled trash can,
a fist forces full
into the ground
pulling tears with glass around.

Pressure makes things grow
like a diamond,
crude,
and rough,
and sharp.

PRESSURE MAKES THINGS

GROW LIKE A DIAMOND,

CRUDE + ROUGH + SHARP.

I WILL   DISSAPOINT YOU

& YOU WILL   WISH   FOR   MORE   OF IT.

I will be angry.
I will be funny
in all the wrong ways.
I will be a box
filled with your
most valuable wishes,
with a hole burnt in the bottom
slowly leaking pieces and kisses.

I will disapoint you
and you will wish for
more of it.

I CARE   TOO   MUCH

ABOUT

HOW   LITTLE   YOU   DO.

I HOPE YOU ARE

AS GOOD WITH YOUR MOUTH

AS YOU ARE WITH YOUR WORDS.

I AM THIS HAPPY,

YOU CAN BE THIS HAPPY.

BEAUTIFUL

HAS   TEN   THOUSAND

FACES.

YOU   HAVE

ONE.

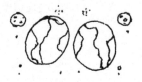

TWO   UNIVERSES

WATCH   FROM   AFAR

DESTROYING   PLANETS

TEARING   WORLDS   APART.

You have pieces of galaxies
trapped in your hair.
Your eyes are moons
I can not help but stare.

We are not people.
We are planets.
We are bigger and deeper
than our bodies allow.

Two universes watch from afar
destroying planets
tearing worlds apart.

just to find eachother at
the center of it all

Sometimes you gotta get used

to hanging out all alone,

+ sometimes you gotta get down with

loving yourself + loving your soul.

AS THE WORLD GROWS QUIET

I AM LEFT WITH WHISPERS OF you,

THAT SCREAM AT THE MOON.

YOU ARE MY HEART
   FULL OF BLOOD,

YOU ARE MY LUNGS
   FULL OF BREATH,

YOU ARE MY LIFE
   FULL OF LOVE.

I LIKE YOU

IN WORDS

I CAN'T EXPLAIN.

I STILL REMEMBER

THE LAST TIME

YOU FELL OUT

OF MY MOUTH,

LIKE THE TEETH

THAT YOU GREW.

METAPHORS FOR OUR LOVE:

BIG SWEATERS

KEEP WARM THOUGHTS

IN COLD WEATHER.

MORNING LIGHT

+ DIRTY THOUGHTS

KEEP ME UP ALL NIGHT.

I PROMISE I WOULD
STILL LOVE YOU,
EVEN IF SOCIETY
DIDN'T PRESSURE ME TO,

THE REASON YOU LOOK SO GOOD

WHEN YOU WAKE UP,

IS BECAUSE I MISSED YOU

ALL NIGHT LONG.

I LOVE HOW YOUR SMELL LINGERS

ON EVERY PILLOW THAT WE SHARE.

I'M ALWAYS SLEEPING WITH YOUR FINGERS

TRACING PUZZLES THROUGH MY HAIR.

SICK TO MY STOMACH

FROM ALL MY BUTTERFLIES

YOU MADE ME SPIT UP.

I AM STILL

SO SURPRISED

BY THE EMPTINESS

I FIND.

LETS JUST ENJOY

OUR TIME TOGETHER

BEFORE I HAVE TO

GO HOME.

I WILL HOLD

ALL YOUR PAIN;

ALL YOUR THINGS.

IF YOU   NEED   ME

I   AM   HERE,

IF YOU   NEED   SPACE

I   AM   GONE.

The solution to life's problems
is finding something
or someone
to make you not care about
the solution to life's problems.

This can be anything
and constantly changing.

THE SOLUTION TO

LIFES PROBLEMS

IS FINDING SOMETHING

OR

SOMEONE TO MAKE YOU

NOT CARE ABOUT THE

SOLUTION TO LIFES PROBLEMS.

YOU WERE MY CATALYST

TO A BETTER LOVE,

SO HERE I AM BURNING UP.

You are gasoline
on a patch of dirt and dust,
we have no reason to be
but we are just enough.
You were my catalyst
to a better love,
so here I am burning up.

TEMPT   ME.

EVEN   AFTER   I   TELL   YOU

I   LOVE   YOU.

MAKE   ME   REMEMBER

OVER   &   OVER

THE   REASON   I   CAN'T   SLEEP

WITHOUT   YOU   THERE.

TANGLED   UP   IN   TWO

LIKE   I   AM   TANGLED   UP   IN   YOU.

Hate. Hate. Hate.
It is too late.
I am done
taking hate for granted,
I do not want to live life
with a minute more of it.
I am going to speak love
until your heart fills up
or your ears fall off.

I AM GOING TO SPEAK LOVE

UNTIL YOUR HEART FILLS UP

OR YOUR EARS FALL OFF.

MY FAVOURITE SONG

IS YOU

BREATHING BESIDE ME.

I love the sound of rain on glass.
I love the sound of
my head in the grass.
I love the sound I play
in my head
as you wander slowly towards me.
My favourite song
is you breathing beside me.

I DON'T MISS YOU.
WHY?
BECAUSE YOU ARE ALWAYS WITH ME.
YOU'RE AN IDIOT.

I CAN'T DO ANYTHING

FOR 'LOOKS',

MY EYES JUST DON'T

LOOK THAT WAY.

There you go running,
there I go coming.
Following you through pieces of glass.
Following you like a warning sign.
I wanted to get lost in the thought of you.
I got left behind.

I WANTED TO GET LOST

IN THE THOUGHT OF YOU,

BUT I GOT LEFT BEHIND.

CAN I SLEEP WITH YOU TONIGHT?

THE DARKNESS ALWAYS SEEMED TO BE

AFRAID OF YOUR LOVING EYES.

METAPHORS   FOR   OUR   LOVE:

I   AM   A   TURTLE.

I   AM   A   BLUE JAY.

I   AM   A   LITTLE BEAR   CUB.

I   AM   A   TERRIBLE   MONSTER
NOBODY   WILL   EVER   LOVE.

I remember the way you talked about my face,
I can not forget the way
your fingers traced my brain.
You said I had a way with words
but you sent me away.
You still kept saying my eyes were beautiful,
but I never saw you look in them.

YOU KEPT SAYING

MY EYES WERE BEAUTIFUL,

BUT I NEVER SAW YOU

LOOK IN THEM.

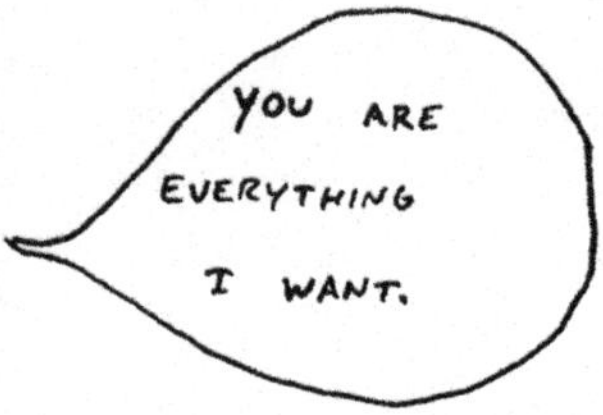
YOU ARE EVERYTHING I WANT.

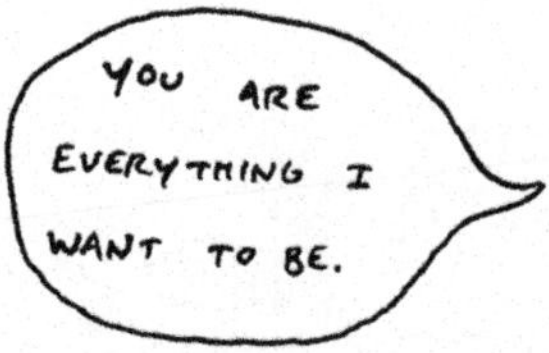
YOU ARE EVERYTHING I WANT TO BE.

I don't care
who you are,
or who you were
now or before.
Your life started
when you met me,
and my life started
when I met you.

THERE IS MORE TO LIFE
THAN LOVE,
BUT I DON'T CARE MUCH
FOR THAT STUFF.

A Letter From the Editor:

I just wanted to thank you for being here and reading my thoughts on love. These are by all means not at all the entirety of my thoughts on love, and not a complete dive into what I think on the subject. I would need a much longer book to tell you all of my thoughts, and if you are good maybe one day I will finish that book. These are simply the beginning thoughts on understanding one of the most complicated and complex topics I have not been able to begin to devour in our world. Love can be found in every single thing we deal with. It can relate to yourself, a shoe, to your animal, to someone you have a crush on when you are three years old, or when you are thirty-six years old and married with a two three year olds. Love can pertain to someone you hate. Love can be found in an ant or the process of building a ten thousand foot skyscraper. Love is mixed into almost every human emotion and if it is not, it can be.

I am not here to tell you I know anything for sure, and this book is not and never was supposed to answer any questions, but I love if it did. This book was simply written as any of my other pieces of poetry have been written. The simplicity in my words, the sometimes lack of direction, the open-endedness, it is all purposeful and used to help you create your own thoughts and thinking on subjects we are all still and maybe always hoping to answer.

I am not an expert, and you are not an expert, nobody is an expert alone. We need each other and to love in order to answer any question. That is the purpose of my book, and my work. I want to start the conversation, to ask the question, to propose the theory; I never had the answers, just a few thoughts on love.

THESE WORDS ARE OURS;

YOU MAY BORROW THEM BUT BRING THEM BACK.

Made in the USA
Monee, IL
17 June 2020

33785496R00095